Enhancing Therap

This is a workbook for children. It is also meant to provide children with resources to assist them in the Resourcing (relaxation) Phase. Any resemblance to existing persons is entirely coincidental.

Copyright © 2024 by Dr. Treva Jones,
DSW, LCSW, MSW

All rights reserved. No parts of this book may be reproduced in any way without the express consent of the copyright owner aside from the use of quotations for book reviews or academic purposes.

First Edition August 2024

Cover Illustration/Veronica Iezzi
Editors/Robert Jones & Jdia Jones

Published by Dr. Treva Jones
www.trevajonesassociates.com
treva@trevajonesassociates.com

Preface

This book is dedicated to therapists who are curious about Eye Movement Desensitization and Reprocessing (EMDR). Children everywhere need access to trauma-informed care. Thank you for showing up for them. They need us.

These resources and tools can be used as forms of expressive arts, social-emotional learning (SEL), and any other opportunity that allows children, adolescents, and teens to relax their nervous systems.

To the Children - Continue to express your ideas, thoughts, feelings, beliefs, and pain. Someone will listen. Keep hope. Children everywhere need something to believe in and something to look forward to. Keep growing.
Dr. Treva Jones,
DSW, LCSW, MSW

Have you ever asked yourself:

What is a thought?

What is a feeling?

What is a mood?

What is an emotion?

What is a body sensation?

What does negative mean?

What does positive mean? Since you might be interested, let's look it up. Maybe we can Google it.

Table of Contents

Children's Manual

What is EMDR? .... Page 1

Creating a Supportive Environment .... Page 3

Accessing Positive Emotions Through Play .... Page 5

Managing Overwhelming Emotions .... Page 7

Strengthening Coping Skills .... Page 8

Empowerment & Safety .... Page 10

Focus on Diversity .... Page 11

Preparing for Future Phases .... Page 12

BLS & DAS Methods .... Page 13

Activities & Exercises .... Page 14

Therapist's Manual

What is EMDR? .... Page 43

Creating a Supportive Environment .... Page 44

Accessing Positive Emotions Through Play .... Page 45

Managing Overwhelming Emotions .... Page 46

Strengthening Coping Skills .... Page 47

Empowerment & Safety .... Page 48

Focus on Diversity .... Page 49

Preparing for Future Phases .... Page 50

BLS & DAS Methods .... Page 51

What is EMDR?

EMDR is like a special game that helps kids feel better when they think about something really scary or sad. Imagine if you had a bad dream about a monster, and every time you remember it, it makes you feel scared. An EMDR therapist, who is like a friendly helper, will ask you to think about that monster while doing some fun movements, like following their finger as it moves back and forth or tapping your hands together in a silly way. This helps your brain clean up those scary feelings, just like how we clean our toys to make our room nice and tidy!

What is EMDR?

When you're playing this game with the therapist, your brain gets better at understanding those scary thoughts and making them seem smaller and less frightening. It's like turning down the volume on a loud TV so it doesn't hurt your ears anymore! After practicing EMDR, you might find that thinking about the bad dream feels easier and not as scary. You can start feeling brave again, just like being a superhero facing down the monster! Isn't that exciting?

Questions to Think About:
1. What helps you relax?
2. How often can you relax?

02

Creating A Supportive Environment

Okay! So, you know how sometimes we feel nervous or angry about things that happened? Well, EMDR therapists are like happy helpers who work with kids to make them feel better! They help kids feel safe by listening to them and using fun games. It's kind of like having a super fun playdate where you can share your feelings while doing cool activities that you can enjoy!

Imagine making art with colors, playing with board games, or even costumes and dress up! These activities help kids think about nice places in their mind where they can be calm—like a cozy pillow fort or a sunny beach. It's like when you pretend to be in a cool adventure story! The therapists want to make sure every kid feels heard and understood, just like when you tell your best friend a secret and they really listen.

Creating A Supportive Environment

And guess what? You can also do things like dancing or make crafts while talking about your feelings! It turns into an awesome adventure where you learn about yourself and what makes you happy. So, it's all about having fun while feeling better—just like playing your favorite game but with extra love and care! Isn't that exciting?

Questions to Think About:
1. Picture a fun playdate where you share your feelings.
2. Recall feeling sad or scared. How about discussing it?

04

Accessing Positive Emotions Through Play

To create a supportive environment To help kids feel happy and calm, therapists like to use fun activities. They might use things like drawing, coloring, musical instruments, playing with kinetic sand, and finger puppets. These activities help kids find peaceful places in their minds, whether they're real or make-believe.

Here are more fun games like hopscotch, making masks, bubbles, and bracelets, coloring T-shirts, and telling stories with characters like the ones in video games. These activities help kids feel safe and work through their tough memories.

Accessing Positive Emotions Through Play

Some other fun things to do are gardening, ball throwing, cooking, making bows, and digital storytelling by creating digital stories using apps or software and integrating text, images, and sounds.

Questions to Think About:
1. How can games help kids feel calm and happy?
2. Think of stories that you can express your feelings.

06

Managing Overwhelming Emotions

To manage overwhelming emotions, EMDR therapists help kids like you learn how to handle big feelings. They teach you ways to calm down and feel better when you're feeling upset, scared, sad, or angry. These therapists show you safe and manageable techniques to deal with your emotions.

For example, they might teach you how to take deep breaths, think of happy thoughts, or do fun activities to relax. For example, they might teach you how to pretend to smell cookies, blow out birthday candles, and breathe. You'll learn to recognize when these big feelings start and how to handle them so they don't feel so overwhelming. By practicing these skills, you'll start to feel more in control of your emotions and much happier. This way, you can face tough situations with confidence and calmness.

Questions to Think About:
1. How can I calm down when I feel upset?
2. What are my feelings telling me?

Strengthening Coping Skills

To strengthen your coping skills, a therapist helps you feel better by teaching you ways to stay calm. For example, they might show you how to take deep breaths when you feel upset. They also teach you to think about positive thoughts or do fun activities that make you feel good. You may learn new words to describe your feelings, like "happy," "sad," "angry," or "scared." Notice how your body respond when you think about these feelings.

This helps you understand your emotions better and talk about them. Even when you're not in therapy, you can use these skills to manage your feelings. By practicing these techniques, you'll get better at handling tough situations and feel more in control of your emotions. This makes it easier to stay calm, relaxed, and peaceful.

Questions to Think About:
1. What helps me feel calm and happy?
2. How can I handle tough situations better?

Empowerment & Safety

To help you feel stronger and safer, an EMDR therapist works with you to create a supportive and trusting environment. They use special methods, called trauma-informed principles, to help you feel less overwhelmed by negative thoughts, emotions, and feelings, which makes you feel more secure. The therapist teaches you how to replace those unhelpful thoughts with positive and helpful ones, so you feel more in control of your emotions.

Empowerment & Safety

Therapists help you see yourself and your abilities in a positive way, boosting your confidence and self-esteem. The therapist also encourages you to think in ways that build resilience and strength. By practicing these techniques, you learn to handle tough situations more easily and maintain a sense of calm and control in your everyday life. This can help you face challenges with a positive attitude and feel better about yourself overall.

Questions to Think About:
1. How can I replace negative thoughts with positive ones?
2. What helps me feel more in control and confident?

Focus on Diversity

To focus on diversity, EMDR therapists help you get care that fits who you are and where you come from. They make sure your treatment understands your unique experiences, like your race, gender, and background, which helps you heal better.

They create a safe and welcoming space where you feel included and understood. The therapist uses special methods just for you, helping you become stronger and feel more confident. They also help you get closer to your family and become more involved in your community. This personalized care helps you feel supported and empowered as you work through your feelings and experiences.

Questions to Think About:
1. How can my therapist understand my unique experiences?
2. How can I feel more included and understood?

Preparing for Future Phases

To prepare for future sessions, an EMDR therapist helps you learn ways to handle stress and tough experiences. They teach you how to manage big feelings that come from things that happened as you grew up. The therapist gives you tools to help you understand and control your emotions, like doing a big clean-up inside your mind.

This helps you feel better about what's going on in your life. You'll learn to use different tools that work best for you, just like picking the right tool from a toolbox when you need it. These tools help you stay calm, manage your body and emotions, and feel safe and supported during your sessions and beyond.

Questions to Think About:
1. What tools help me stay calm?
2. How can I manage my big feelings better?

BLS & DAS Methods

Dual Attention Stimulus (DAS [fast]) in EMDR therapy helps you deal with scary memories by using both sides of your brain at the same time. For example, you might follow a moving object with your eyes, listen to sounds that go back and forth in your ears, or feel taps on your hands. Doing these things together makes those scary memories feel less intense and easier to handle.

BLS & DAS Methods

Bilateral Stimulation (BLS [slow]) is a special kind of rhythm. It involves using things like alternating taps, sounds, or eye movements to calm your body and help you process memories. This technique helps you feel less upset by those memories and reduces your anxiety. It also helps you focus better and feel more in control. Imagine it like having special tools that help your brain work through tough memories more easily, making them less scary and overwhelming. With BLS, you can feel calmer and stronger while working through difficult emotions.

Here are 8+ ways to BLS:

Butterfly Taps	Swaying
Leg Taps	Pulling
Angel Hugs	Climbing
Eye Movements	Swimming
Marching	Jogging
Painting	Running (Or running in place)
Drawing	

Questions to Think About:
1. How can following a moving object help my brain?
2. How do alternating taps make scary memories less intense?

How Bothered Am I?
Worksheet & Activity

When certain events happen to us, sometimes it might make us feel bad. Some situations might make us feel angry, sad, or scared. These emotions cause us to feel bothered. This worksheet will help you express yourself and your feelings.

Think of a situation that happened, and using the exercises on the next few pages, share how bothered it made you feel. You can also decorate your own chart! If anything bothers you, be sure to bring this up to your EMDR therapist.

1. Describe a situation where you felt emotional.

   _____
   _____
   _____

2. How did you feel better after the situation?

   _____
   _____
   _____

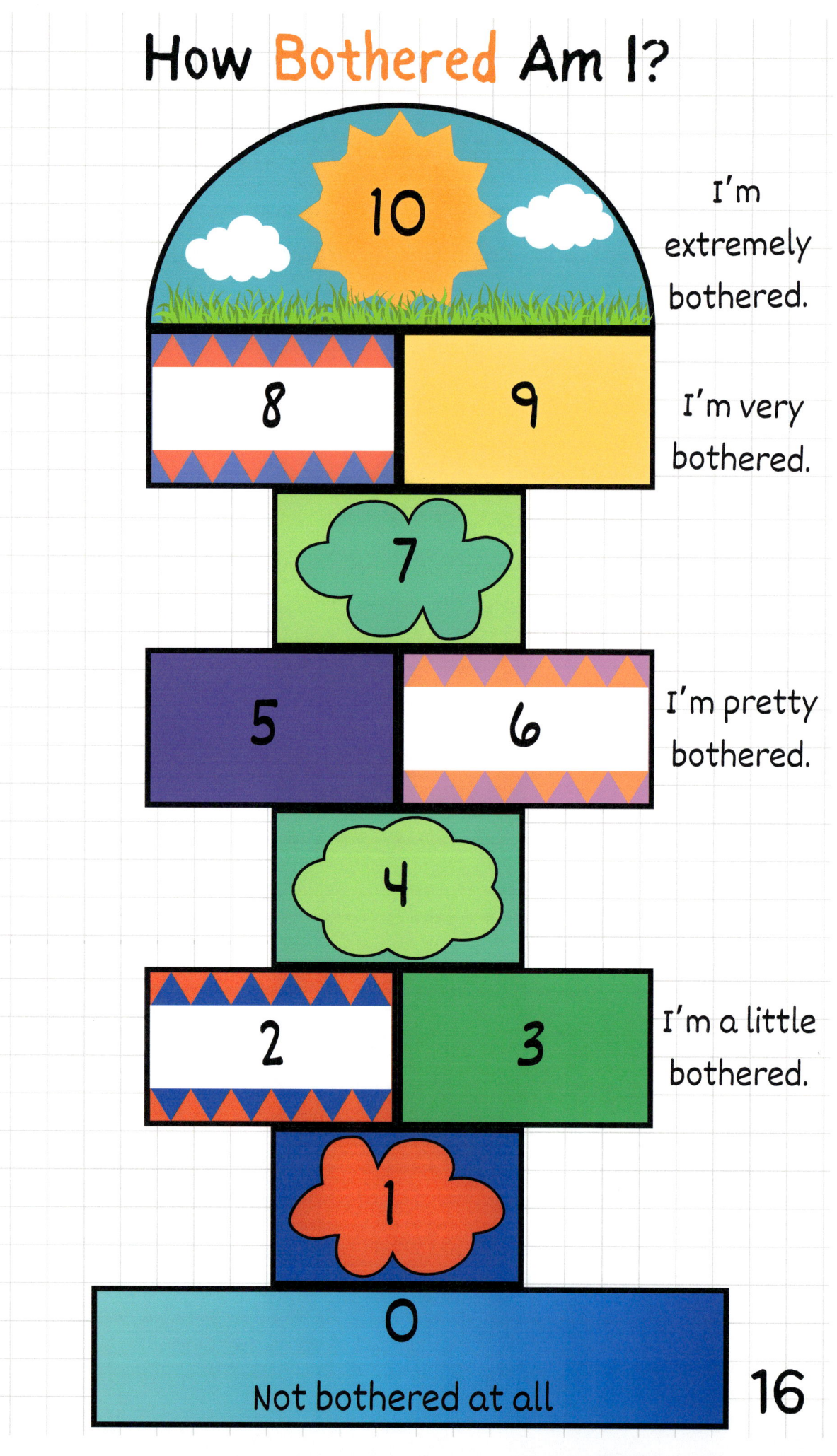

How Bothered Am I?
DIY Chart

Date: _____

Bothersome Thing: _____

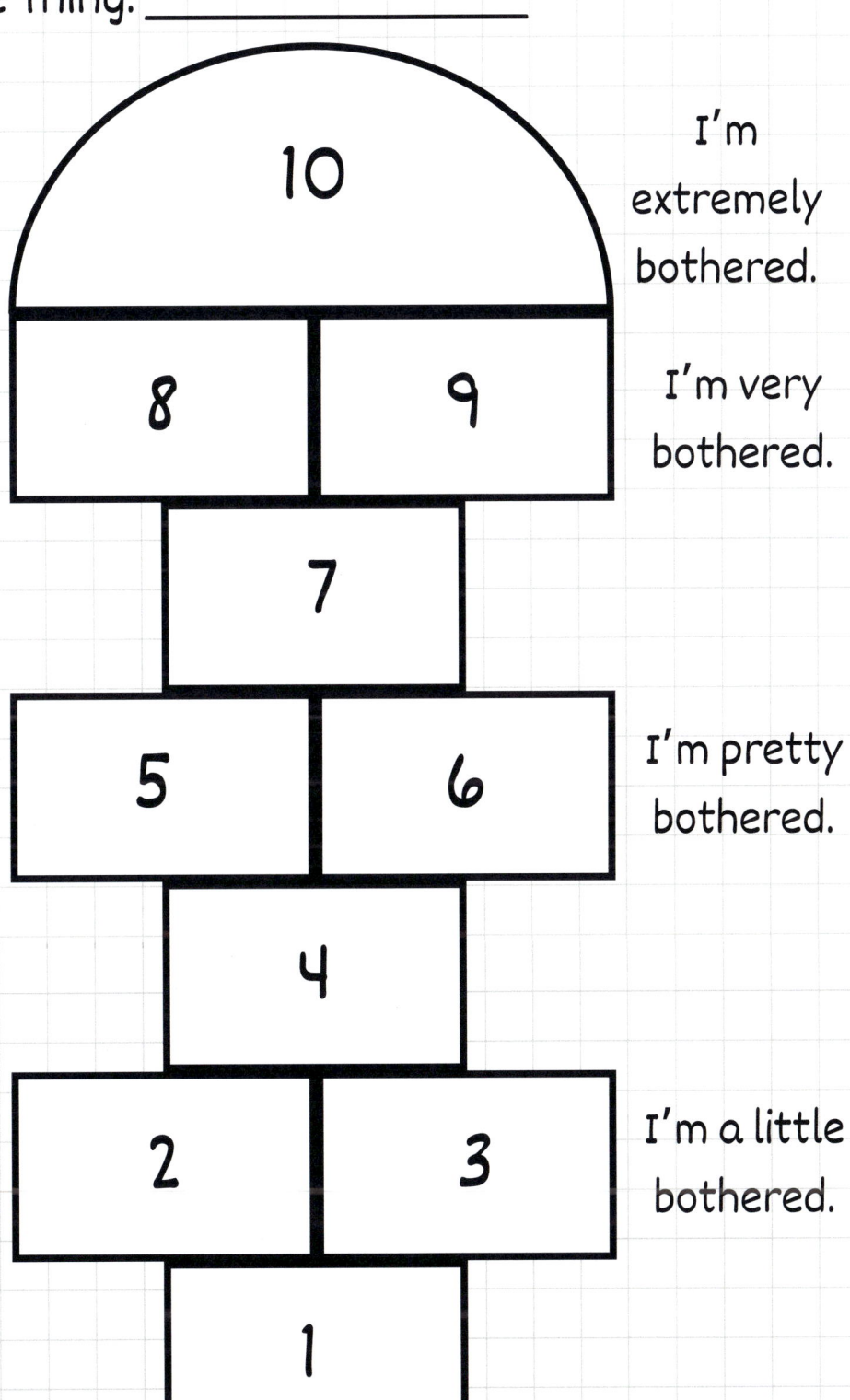

- 10 — I'm extremely bothered.
- 8, 9 — I'm very bothered.
- 7
- 5, 6 — I'm pretty bothered.
- 4
- 2, 3 — I'm a little bothered.
- 1
- 0 — Not bothered at all

17

How True Is This for Me Right Now? Worksheet & Activity

When we say positive things, sometimes we don't entirely believe what we say. Often, you might say "I feel okay", but it doesn't always feel true. It might not feel true in our heart because it aches. It might not feel true in our stomach because we get butterflies.

In this exercise, we are going to explore some of our positive thoughts and beliefs how true it feels to us in the moment. Be sure to bring up this exercise to your EMDR therapist.

1. List some positive thoughts or beliefs that you think about.

_____

_____

_____

2. How do you feel thinking about these thoughts or beliefs?

_____

_____

_____

18

How True is This for Me Right Now?

7 — I believe it and it is true.

6 — I really believe it.

5 — I am starting to believe it.

4 — I'm right in the middle.

3 — I am trying to believe.

2 — I don't entirely believe, but I'm hopeful.

1 — I don't believe that this is true.

How True is This for Me Right Now?
DIY Chart

Date: _____

Positive Thought/Belief: _____

7 — I believe it and it is true.

6 — I really believe it.

5 — I am starting to believe it.

4 — I'm right in the middle.

3 — I am trying to believe.

2 — I don't entirely believe, but I'm hopeful.

1 — I don't believe that this is true.

20

How Am I Feeling Today?
Worksheet & Activity

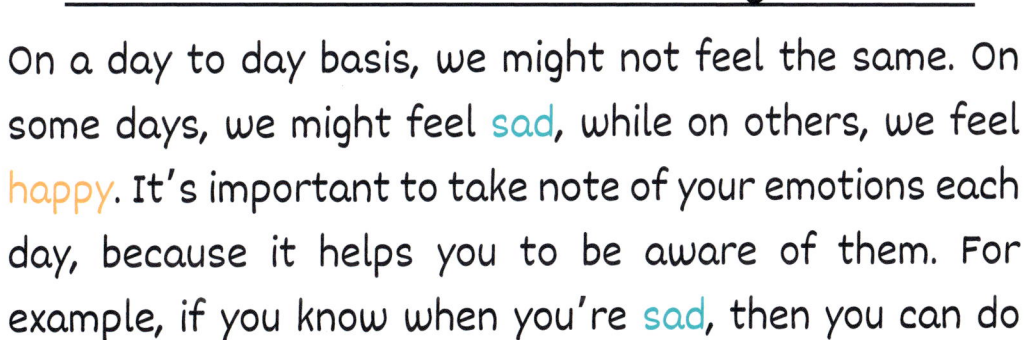

On a day to day basis, we might not feel the same. On some days, we might feel sad, while on others, we feel happy. It's important to take note of your emotions each day, because it helps you to be aware of them. For example, if you know when you're sad, then you can do some of the activities you enjoy so you feel <u>better</u>.

In this exercise, we are going to keep track of our emotions with a variety of charts provided on the next few pages.

1. What do you do to help you feel better on a bad day?

_____

_____

_____

2. What makes a good day?

_____

_____

_____

 # How Am I Feeling Today?
Weekly Activity Reference Key

Here are the emotions that might be needed for the <u>weekly</u> emotion chart.

Confused  When you're unable to think clearly.

Angry  When you have strong negative feelings.

Shy  When you're uncomfortable with other people.

Sad  When you're feeling down.

Worried  When you feel troubled.

Normal  When you feel like how you usually do.

Scared  When you feel afraid.

Happy  When you feel joy.

Tired  When you feel sleepy or lack energy.

Excited  When you feel thrilled.

How Am I Feeling Today?
DIY Weekly Chart

Day of the Week	I'm Feeling...	What Happened?
Sunday		
Monday		
Tuesday		
Wednesday		
Thursday		
Friday		
Saturday		

 How Am I Feeling Today?

Monthly Activity Reference Key

Here are the emotions that might be needed for the <u>monthly</u> emotion chart.

24

The jar contains special circles that will help you feel relaxed and feel good by thinking about positive memories or doing fun relaxation activities.

Pick a number from the jar and do the exercise, then color the circle.

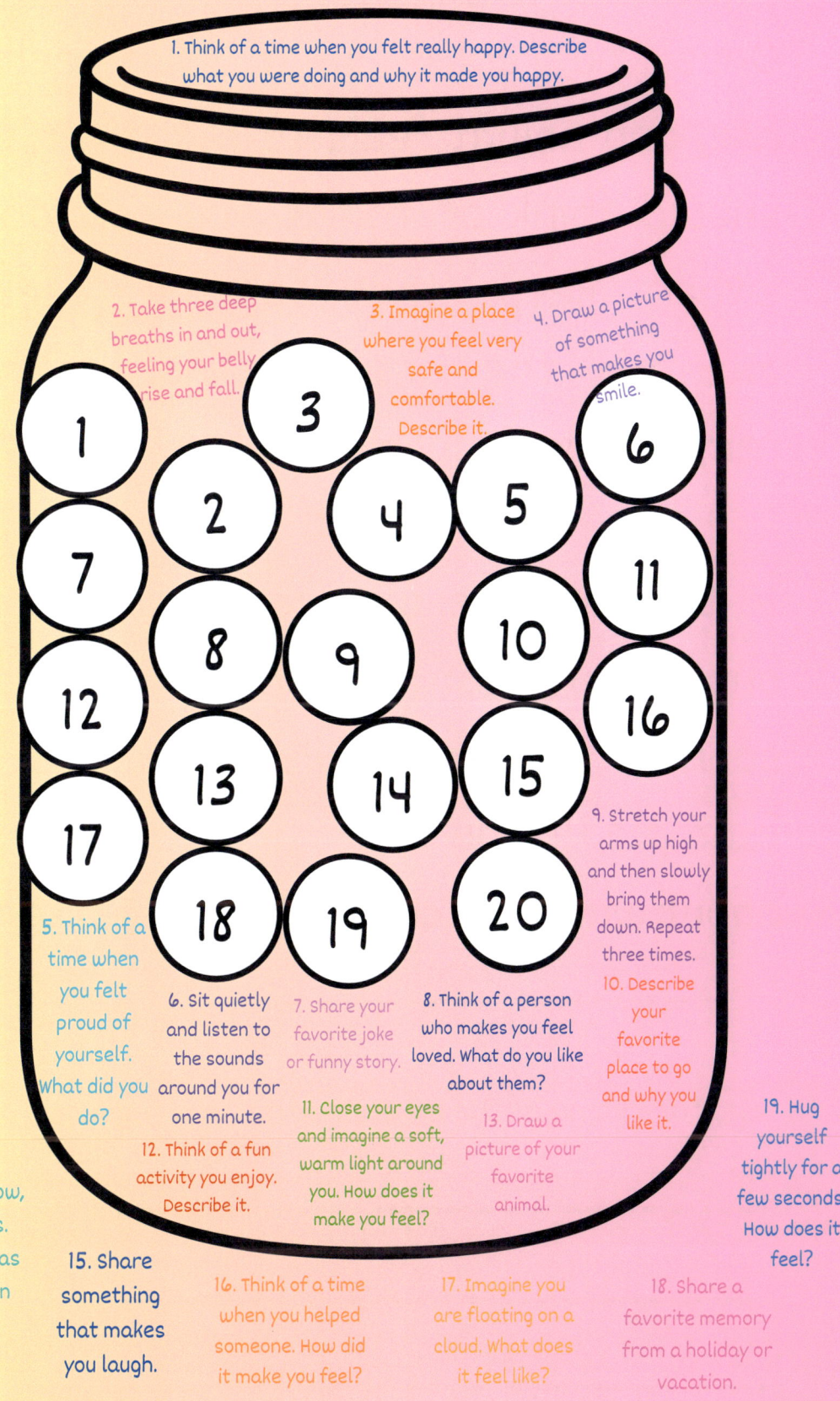

1. Think of a time when you felt really happy. Describe what you were doing and why it made you happy.
2. Take three deep breaths in and out, feeling your belly rise and fall.
3. Imagine a place where you feel very safe and comfortable. Describe it.
4. Draw a picture of something that makes you smile.
5. Think of a time when you felt proud of yourself. What did you do?
6. Sit quietly and listen to the sounds around you for one minute.
7. Share your favorite joke or funny story.
8. Think of a person who makes you feel loved. What do you like about them?
9. Stretch your arms up high and then slowly bring them down. Repeat three times.
10. Describe your favorite place to go and why you like it.
11. Close your eyes and imagine a soft, warm light around you. How does it make you feel?
12. Think of a fun activity you enjoy. Describe it.
13. Draw a picture of your favorite animal.
14. Take five slow, deep breaths. Count to four as you breathe in and out.
15. Share something that makes you laugh.
16. Think of a time when you helped someone. How did it make you feel?
17. Imagine you are floating on a cloud. What does it feel like?
18. Share a favorite memory from a holiday or vacation.
19. Hug yourself tightly for a few seconds. How does it feel?
20. Think of something you are really good at. What is it?

25

Things I Can Do with My Feelings Worksheet & Activity

Once you realize what your feelings are, and how it feels to feel them, you should think of things you can do to either keep the positive feeling, maintain the okay feeling, or help remove the negative feeling.

In this exercise, we are going to figure out what we can do with our feelings as soon as we realize what they are. For example, if you are sad, you can think about what you can do to feel better.

1. What are some of the emotions that you feel each day?

_____

_____

_____

Things I Can Do with My Feelings
DIY Chart

When I Am Feeling Good

I can...

_____

_____

_____

When I Am Feeling Okay

I can...

_____

_____

When I Am Feeling Down

I can...

_____

_____

27

Feelings
Word Search

```
L A J F T R S A N S
O B N O O O S N E C
N H Z N Y V A G R U
E M O K O F D R V R
L X S P B Y U Y O I
Y B C K E H E L U O
V O A I H F A D S U
F R R L T Q U P E S
T E E R C E B L P H
I D D K M Z D P D Y
```

Angry	Curious	Hopeful	Nervous
Annoyed	Excited	Joyful	Sad
Bored	Happy	Lonely	Scared

Relaxing Things To Do
Word Search

```
E N A P P I N G S T
X F L D A N C I N G
E P L B A K I N G H
R P A I N T I N G M
C V O P L A Y I N G
I A S I N G I N G L
S C O O K I N G E P
I P X P G A M I N G
N F D R A W I N G N
G R E A D I N G W O
```

Baking   Drawing   Napping   Reading
Cooking   Exercising   Painting   Singing
Dancing   Gaming   Playing

Holidays
Word Search

```
T E E I H R T W T R R R N
E M R L A B O R D A Y H K
G T H D L D A C I W L N S
A A R G L A Y A D K L M N
L S K Y O E A S T E R R N
T Y N O W A N I I A E S S
N E W Y E A R S S M S S U
A A B O E L A V O S T O N
L T H A N K S G I V I N G
W R J U N E T E E N T H L
V E T E R A N S D A Y A N
T Y A D L A I R O M E M Y
E C H R I S T M A S A D L
```

Christmas   Juneteenth   MLK Day
Easter   Labor Day   New Years
Halloween   Memorial Day   Thanksgiving
Veterans Day

30

Tree of Reflection Worksheet & Activity

Sometimes when we're feeling bad, we might not know why. A bad feeling isn't always explainable, but sometimes we might be able to figure it out.

In this exercise, we are going to sit with ourselves and think about a problem that's causing us to feel down. Then, we're going to think about a <u>solution</u>.

_____

1. How can you identify what makes you unhappy?

_____
_____
_____

Tree of Reflection
DIY Chart

What is the problem?

_____
_____
_____
_____
_____
_____

How does it affect you?

_____
_____
_____
_____
_____
_____

What's the solution?

_____
_____
_____
_____
_____
_____

Five Things That I...
Worksheet & Activity

When you're feeling down, you might find it helpful to think about some of the things that you like, or some of the things that make you feel better.

In this exercise, we are going to identify <u>five</u> things that we like, and <u>five</u> things that we can do to feel better.

Five Things That I Like

Five Things I Can Do To Feel Better

Five Things That I Like
DIY Chart

1. I like _____

2. I like _____

3. I like _____

4. I like _____

5. I like _____

Five Things That I Can Do To Feel Better
DIY Chart

1. I can _____

2. I can _____

3. I can _____

4. I can _____

5. I can _____

Rainbow of Hope
Worksheet & Activity

In this exercise, we are going to rise above our circumstances. Using the rainbow of hope, we will be able to rise above the clouds of negativity and remain hopeful. Feel free to add your own colors to the rainbow on the next page.

Hope

My Sadness

My Stress

36

Rainbow of Hope
DIY Chart

Hope

My Safety Umbrella Worksheet & Activity

Despite how hard we try, the rainclouds of life will still try to rain down on us. However, we can stay safe by using our safety umbrella, which keeps us dry.

In this exercise, we will use the next page to color our own safety umbrella and share what it protects us from.

My Safety Umbrella
DIY Chart

My Safety Umbrella
Protects Me From...

_____
_____
_____
_____

My Positivity Flower Worksheet & Activity

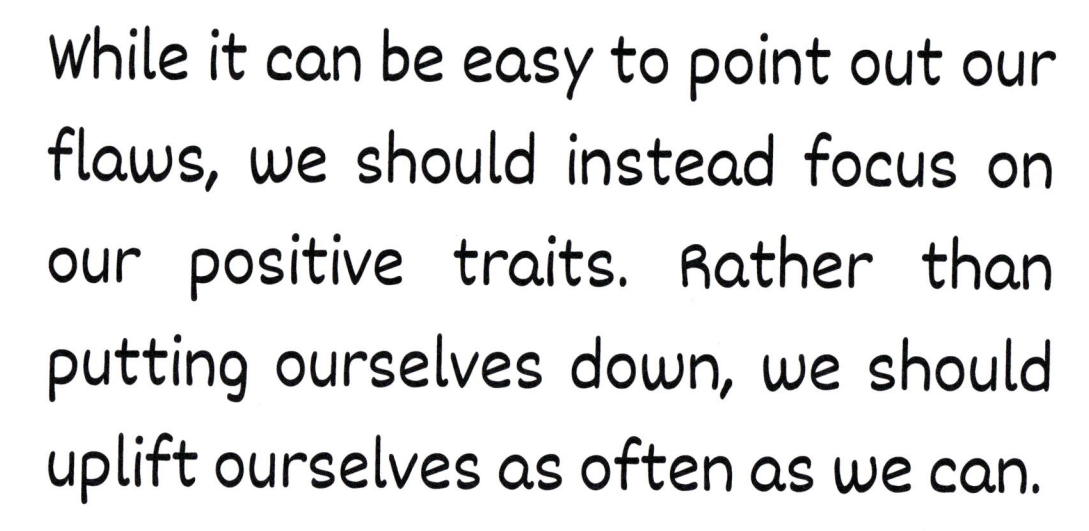

While it can be easy to point out our flaws, we should instead focus on our positive traits. Rather than putting ourselves down, we should uplift ourselves as often as we can.

In this exercise, we will use the positivity flower on the next page. We will write down <u>five</u> positive things that we are grateful for. For example, "I am kind."

1. How often do you tell yourself positive things?

_____

_____

_____

My Positivity Flower
DIY Chart

- I am _____
- I am _____
- I am _____
- I am _____
- I am _____
- I am _____

My Positive Traits

Body Sensations
DIY Chart

Date: _____

What feelings do you feel? _____

Where is it located in your body? _____

Head

Hand   Arm   Arm   Hand

Chest

Tummy

Leg   Leg

Foot   Foot

Therapist's Manual

What is EMDR?

EMDR is a psychotherapy technique used to help individuals process traumatic or other disturbing life experiences (Shapiro; 2018). It may involve movement of the eyes, tapping or other BLS/DAS processes provided by a trained professional. The various forms of bilateral stimulation are used to help process and reduce disturbing or traumatic memories and their emotional impact. It is a type of therapy that helps children to feel better after something really scary or upsetting has happened or may be happening in the future.

For example, a therapist may ask a child to think about an upsetting memory while doing simple movements like following a light bar, marching, gorilla taps or simply following therapist's fingers or a magic wand. The processing helps situations to seem less scary. If a child had a really awful nightmare, experience flashbacks, or had a bad dream, the therapist might ask the child to bring up the memory from storage, then engage the child in bilateral movements such as left and right, back and forward up and down. The child follows. Their brain is assisted with processing and the child's brain begins to understand better and make it a little less scary reducing thoughts, urges, triggers, memories, body sensations and negative core beliefs. EMDR is like spring cleaning the child's room, brain, body sensations, thoughts and nervous system. The presenting problem or situation becomes less and less scary in their mind causing them to not have to feel afraid anymore and begin to feel much better.

Creating A Supportive Environment

To create a supportive environment, EMDR therapists work with children to help them feel grounded, heard, seen, understood, supported increasing their feelings of safety and comfortability. This is called resourcing (Kiessling, 2005; Kiessling 2024 June edition).

Therapists use fun interactive techniques that are simple and super engaging to make each session enjoyable. Within this book, I hope you get to feel the enjoyment of using the provided resources to help you engage children with interactive tools that help children express thoughts, feelings and emotional regulation more easily. This helps to guide processing more easily and is soothing.

Accessing Positive Emotions Through Play

To access positive emotions through play, therapists may use various activities such as art, AI art, coloring, drawing, Lego blocks, playdough, magic carpets, and finger puppets to interactively engage children and help them find calm and peaceful places, whether real or imagined.

Recently, I have found success in engaging children with activities such as hopscotch, mask-making, jewelry-making (creating rings and bracelets), coloring T-shirts, and storytelling through the creation of avatars similar to video game characters. These activities help children safely work through traumatic memories and recover from their experiences.

Other activities include sensory play with sand or water guided imaginative play, music and dance sessions, scavenger hunts. My discovery has been engaging children with activities like virtual nature walks to explore and collect leaves, storytelling through creating comic strips, interactive board games, and mindfulness exercises tailored for children.

Managing Overwhelming Emotions

EMDR therapists assist children in managing overwhelming emotions by teaching them effective coping skills and relaxation techniques (Shapiro, 2018). They guide youth in processing emotions within their "window of tolerance" (Siegel, 1999), helping them recognize and understand feelings of upset, fear, sadness, and anger. This approach enables children to navigate intense emotions more effectively, fostering emotional regulation and resilience. Through these therapeutic techniques, children learn to identify their emotional triggers and develop healthy responses, contributing to their overall emotional well-being and mental health.

Strengthening Coping Skills

To strengthen coping skills, A therapist helps youth strengthen coping skills by teaching deep breathing, grounding, and visualization techniques. They learn to use these resources to relax their bodies and feel more in control of their emotions and triggers, both during and between therapy sessions. By understanding feeling words and practicing enjoyable activities, they build resilience and handle difficult life challenges more effectively (Shapiro, 2018). This approach empowers them to manage situations better and develop stronger emotional regulation skills.

Empowerment & Safety

To increase empowerment and safety, an EMDR therapist helps youth create supportive environments and build trust using trauma-informed principles. This approach reduces unhelpful thoughts and overwhelming feelings, making children feel more secure. Therapists work with children to develop essential self-control skills by teaching them to replace negative thoughts with positive and helpful ones.

They reinforce positive core beliefs, helping children to view themselves and their abilities in a more favorable light. Additionally, therapists encourage preferred ways of thinking that promote resilience and confidence. By practicing these techniques, children learn to handle challenging situations with greater ease and maintain a sense of calm and control in their everyday lives.

Focus on Diversity

To focus on diversity, EMDR Therapists assist youth with receiving personalized, culturally sensitive care that will improve meaningful and effective healing outcomes.

These personalizations include addressing trauma from diverse perspectives, including race, gender, and class, promoting inclusivity (safety and validation), using specialized treatment approaches that are client-specific, fostering resilience, and building empowerment.

EMDR Therapist helps youth to increase family engagement and build community, including in foster families, blended families, and adoptive families, which can be processed through phases 3-7.

Preparing for Future Phases

To prepare for future phases, EMDR Therapist help youth with resourcing as a means to help them live within their body in a way that manages tolerance of stressful and traumatic events backed by negative core beliefs that may have developed during the stages of development.

By equipping young people with ways to regulate their feelings for the emotional job of spring cleaning what is happening inside of their head and within their life experiences – we help young people manage their bodies and emotions in safe and supportive ways using tools they prefer the most. It is like having a toolbox and picking a tool is more useful in a time of need.

BLS & DAS Methods

Dual Attention Stimulus (DAS [Fast]) in EMDR therapy helps process traumatic memories by engaging both sides of the brain with visual, auditory, or tactile stimuli. Typically, this is faster than BLS. For example, you might follow a moving object, listen to alternating sounds, or feel rhythmic tapping. This dual engagement makes distressing memories less intense.

Bilateral Stimulation (BLS [Slow]), a type of DAS, involves alternating stimuli to both sides of the body, calming the nervous system and aiding memory processing. Typically, this is slower than DAS. Types of BLS include eye movements, alternating beeps, and taps. This technique reduces the emotional impact of trauma, soothes anxiety, and improves focus for deeper emotional healing.

Epilogue

Dear Reader,

Thank you for taking the time to read this book. I hope the process was deeply fulfilling. Feel free to reach out to me directly at www.trevajonesassociates.com

Be sure to be on the lookout for more books geared towards children, teens, and adults. I believe that everyone has the opportunity to reach their fullest potential, and I want to ensure that the resources needed are there to assist every child on their journey towards healing.

Take Care,
Dr. Treva Jones

References

Kiessling, R. (2005). Integrating resource development strategies into your EMDR practice. In R. Shapiro (Ed.), EMDR Solutions: Pathways to Healing (pp. 57-87). W W Norton & Co.

Shapiro, F. (2014). The role of eye movement desensitization and reprocessing (EMDR) therapy in medicine: Addressing the psychological and physical symptoms stemming from adverse life experiences. The Permanente Journal, 18(1), 71-77. https://doi.org/10.7812/TPP/13-098

Shapiro, F. (2018). Eye movement desensitization and reprocessing (EMDR) therapy (3rd ed.). Guilford Press.

Made in the USA
Columbia, SC
08 November 2024